Horsforth ·
HMS *Aubrietia,*
Enigma and Ultra

To Alan Turing – designer of the world's first computer, whose genius is best described in the following quotation:

"Sometimes it is the people no one can imagine anything of, who do the things no one can imagine."

and

To the Royal Air Force and Bletchley Park – for teaching me Morse code, telephony, telegraphy and direction finding

Horsforth –
HMS *Aubrietia*,
Enigma and Ultra

Jack Metcalfe

First published in the United Kingdom by
Jack Metcalfe
Yorkshire
England

ISBN 978 1 9164958 5 2

Copyright © Jack Metcalfe 2023
Website HorsforthWarship&Enigma.com
Instagram Instagram.com/horsforth_hms_aubrietia

Design and typesetting by Hugh Hillyard-Parker, Edinburgh, hugh@hillyard.org.uk

Contents

Acknowlegements

The author wishes to acknowledge the following people, whose skills and expertise have in some way contributed to the writing and production of this book.

Hugh Hillyard-Parker – editor and book designer (and Horsforth resident, 1967–1984)

Horsforth Village Museum – especially historian Nancy Di-Dombal for all her teaching on the history of the sponsorship of HMS *Aubrietia*

Residents of Victoria Court, Headingley, Leeds (Author's home) for listening and supporting the author's first lecture on the contents of this book

Royal Air Force – for teaching me the Morse code and the technical know-how of telephony and telegraphy; then sending me to Bletchley Park for further advanced training

Post Office – who ran Bletchley Park in 1958, where I was trained on Direction Finding equipment construction and operating techniques

The National Museum of Computing – for supporting me and inviting me to be their guest speaker on Zoom and in person at a forthcoming event in 2024. Look for dates either on my website (see page iv), and/or the Bletchley website www.tnmoc.org

Finally, to all those enigmatic mathematical cryptanalysts employed by GCHQ, who between them broke the German coded messages, allowing Britain to end the war much sooner

CHAPTER ONE

Introduction

I write to you here today in the month of May 2023 at the age of 84, to outline one of most significant episodes and one of the most compelling stories to be told concerning the Second World War between Germany and Britain.

I was born on 2nd January 1939 in the village of Bramley, Leeds, in West Yorkshire. World War II commenced on the 1st September of that year, so clearly the events I am to write about took place mainly in my formative years; yet I discovered one intriguing association only when I was aged 49.

I lived in Horsforth for 18 years with my family, between 1965 and 1983. The street, called Stanhope Drive, was the Horsforth Memorial Street, with trees lining both sides of the street to commemorate the 211 men and one woman from Horsforth who died in the First World War. Though I was aware of this wartime connection, at the time I didn't realise just what a significant part this village that I called home had played in the Second World War too.

I can confidently state that there are few, if any, people living today whose lives have been touched so directly by the events of this compelling wartime drama as my own.

So I hope you will enjoy coming with me on a fascinating journey which starts in a village called Horsforth, now a suburb of Leeds, but which in 1941 boasted the title 'Britain's largest village'. This proud village sponsored a warship, HMS *Aubrietia*, pictured on the next page, that was to play a key role in making startling discoveries that helped to foil the plans of Nazi Germany.

HMS Aubrietia – key protagonist in the story

The journey then takes us on to Bletchley Park, the home of Britain's secret code-breaking teams, and my own fascinating involvement there in 1958 and again in 2007.

Let the story begin ...

CHAPTER TWO

Horsforth at War

The date is November 1941 and Britain has been at war with Nazi Germany since September 1939. Since the start of the War in 1939, the Royal Navy has not only lost many fighting ships but is also under huge pressure to provide escorts for convoys in the Atlantic bringing in essential supplies. Ships sunk by enemy action have to be replaced. The home country is desperate for financial assistance and decides to turn to its people for a solution. They achieve it by inviting Britain's cities, towns and some villages to sponsor warships.

HORSFORTH WARSHIP WEEK

To do this, they introduce 'Warship Weeks', local campaigns whereby civil communities raise enough money to adopt a Royal Navy warship. The aim is for cities to raise enough to adopt battleships and aircraft carriers, while towns and villages would focus on cruisers and destroyers. Smaller towns and villages would be set a lower figure. Once the target money was saved for the ship, the community would adopt the ship and its crew.

The city of Leeds sponsored the aircraft carrier HMS *Ark Royal* in November 1941, yet only days afterwards the ship was torpedoed and sunk by a German U-Boat in the Mediterranean. Totally enraged by this event, the residents of Leeds launched another fundraising week to sponsor a new *Ark Royal* and by February 1942 the city raised over £7.5 million. The population then was 608,000.

If that was impressive, what happened next was truly astounding. Britain's largest village Horsforth was asked by the War Office to sponsor a corvette, the smallest classification of warships. Unlike its city neighbour, Leeds, Horsforth only had a population of just over 12,600, yet we will now see the impressive achievement it made in just seven days, compared to its neighbouring city.

SPONSORING HMS *AUBRIETIA*

Horsforth Warship Week ran from 15th to 22nd November 1941. The official opening ceremony of the week took place on Saturday 15th November 1941 at the Glenroyal Cinema, and the Horsforth New Choral Society contributed several patriotic songs.

On the Sunday, after a parade from the Horsforth Cenotaph in Fink Hill (pictured on the right), the Princess Royal (Mary, the only daughter of George V) and her husband, the Earl of Harewood (Lord Lieutenant of the West Riding),

HORSFORTH WARSHIP WEEK

NOVEMBER 15th - 22nd
The Signal is Save

OFFICIAL PROGRAMME

The Cenotaph in Fink Hill, Horsforth

attended a service in St Margaret's Church. The Earl presented
an autographed book to 14-year-old, Roland Allanach, who
sang a solo, 'I Vow to Thee My Country'. The Earl took the
salute in front of the Imperial Picture house on Town Street.

How the money was raised

The money to pay for the corvette was raised, through a
variety of different events.

On the 14th November, a Whist Drive and Dance was held
at Broadway Hall (now Bartletts Insurance Co). Tickets were
2s. 6d and dancing went on till 1 am.

A concert was held on the Tuesday evening, 18th
November, and on Wednesday 19th, Mr Arthur Saville
presented prizes for a children's poster competition at
Featherbank School.

Whist drives, Beetle drives, and baby shows were held, and
donated goods were sold – even a lemon was sent home from
Tunisia by one Sgt Appleyard, which was auctioned off.

Schools and Boy Scouts raised money through collecting old papers, pans and pots, and other metal objects. Even the iron railings around Hall Park were cut down and sent to be melted down.

Every day of that week, a travelling notice board was seen displaying the growth of monies raised.

The cost of *Aubrietia* and the total raised

The target for Horsforth's Warship Week was £120,000. This was the total money needed to fund the building of a corvette. Specifically, Horsforth was tasked with sponsoring HMS *Aubrietia*, which had been built by George Brown & Co. Ship Builders in Greenock, Scotland. It had been completed on the 23rd December 1940 and was one of the so-called 'Flower class' vessels of corvettes (because all were named after flowers) and it was given the pendant number K96.

Horsforth people were asked to invest their monies in 'National Savings', which 'The British Government guaranteed'.

They raised in total £241,044 7s 10d, equivalent to £19 per head of the population of Horsforth. In today's money (2023), this is equivalent to nearly £16 million pounds (or over £1200 per person in the village).

By the end of the week the target was reached, and Councillor Willcock sent a telegram to the First Lord of the Admiralty

> 'HM CORVETTE AUBRIETIA BOWT AND PAID FOR. WHAT'S THA WANT NEXT?'

I can only imagine that Willcock knew that the First Lord of the Admiralty was a Yorkshireman and therefore would appreciate the humour of the 'Yorkshire dialect' used within the telegram!

In recognition of the village's achievement during warship week, a plaque (shown here) was presented by the Lords Commissioners of the Admiralty to commemorate the adoption of HMS *Aubrietia*. The is currently on display at Horsforth Museum.

OTHER WARTIME EVENTS IN HORSFORTH

Horsforth women (seen here) worked 12-hour shifts at the Yeadon Avro factory to build Avro Anson trainers and Lancaster bombers.

As a precaution against air raids, the factory was disguised with a grass roof and dummy sheep, which were moved daily, so as to appear from the air as a farm. The factory was never bombed, despite efforts by enemy air reconnaissance planes searching for the site.

Yeadon Tarn, a large lake, was drained, so that the water would not reflect from the air and highlight the surrounding landscape.

Workers at the Avro factory in Yeadon, pictured with a Lancaster bomber

AVRO LANCASTER & WORKERS YEADON 1941-42

Refugee children arrive 1940 from Guernsey

The Channel Islands, near the north coast of France, were the only parts of the British Isles to be occupied by the Germans during the War. In June 1940, just days before the Nazis arrived, 17,000 Guernsey residents were evacuated by ship to the south coast of England, and then moved to towns and cities all over the UK, including a large number to the north of England. This British evacuation included 5,000 schoolchildren who were evacuated with their teachers at very short notice.

Horsforth received 199 of the Guernsey refugees, ranging in age from 2 weeks to 71 years. They turned up at 4 am at the Leeds train station on Monday 28th June 1940. They had been travelling all weekend and many were babies.

The evacuees were taken first to Outwood Lane Chapel, sleeping on the floor until suitable family accommodation was found. For them, Horsforth was to be their home until the liberation of the Channel Islands in May 1945. Coming to Yorkshire from the warmer climes of Guernsey was a shock: for example, most of them had never seen snow before.

Children evacuated from Guernsey arrive in the UK

A Channel Island Association was formed, in Horsforth, to help the evacuees with clothing and other necessities.

REDISCOVERING THE *AUBRIETIA* LINK

It seems that after the war, the achievements of Horsforth's residents in raising the money to pay for a warship were largely forgotten. Understandably, people's minds were focused on other priorities, such as rebuilding the economy and learning to live in peace time.

Over 50 years later, in 1999, a TV programme told of the capture of an enemy submarine. The people of Horsforth discovered that 'their ship', HMS *Aubrietia*, had played a decisive part in the course of the war. Ron Hartley of the Horsforth Historical Society through the local MP, Paul Truswell, contacted the Ministry of Defence to find out whether any of the *Aubrietia* crew could be traced. Several surviving members got in touch and were pleased to know they had not been forgotten.

A plan was then made, with the Town Council, to erect a memorial plaque to celebrate the 60th Anniversary of the event and, with the help and generosity of numerous local organisations and residents, Horsforth raised the money to fund a memorial stone. This was

9

THIS STONE IS TO COMMEMORATE THE ENDEAVOURS OF
THE PEOPLE OF HORSFORTH
AND THE CREW OF HMS AUBRIETIA.

DURING NAVY WEEK IN 1941 HORSFORTH RESIDENTS RAISED
£241,000 TO ADOPT THIS CORVETTE WHICH IN MAY 1941,
TOGETHER WITH HMS BULLDOG AND HMS BROADWAY,
ATTACKED AND DISABLED THE GERMAN SUBMARINE U110 IN
THE NORTH ATLANTIC. THE SUBMARINE'S CREW ABANDONED
THEIR BOAT AND A BOARDING PARTY SUCCESSFULLY
RECOVERED A WORKING ENIGMA CODING MACHINE TOGETHER
WITH OTHER DOCUMENTS. THIS ENABLED THE ALLIED CODE-
BREAKERS TO DECIPHER GERMAN TRANSMISSIONS LEADING
TO THE ULTIMATE DEFEAT OF THE GERMAN NAVY AND
VICTORY IN THE ATLANTIC.

DEDICATED
28ᵗʰ OCTOBER 2001
TO CELEBRATE THE 60ᵗʰ ANNIVERSARY

RE-DEDICATED
16TH OCTOBER 2011
TO CELEBRATE THE 70TH ANNIVERSARY

erected in the Museum grounds and Dedicated on 28th October 2001.

Guests of Honour from the original *Aubrietia* crew were Sir Barry Sheen, Douglas Bacon, Donald Rig, Frank Syred, Len Thompson and Stan Wilson, together with John Pegg from HMS *Bulldog*.

This was preceded by an impressive parade of military and local organisations marching down Town Street to the Museum, led by the Guests of Honour in a veteran car. Twenty organisations were represented, including The Royal Naval Association, The Fleet Air Arm Association, The Fleet Air Armourers Association and the Royal Marines, with flags aloft.

The information about the 2001 Commemoration is reproduced from the booklet, 'From Atlantic to Station X', with grateful thanks to the author, Peter A. Watson (now deceased). It was published by Horsforth Village Historical Society © September 2011, but is sadly now out of print. Book now replaced and renamed 'HMS Aubrietia: The Horsforth Ship', written by Beryl Biggins.

CHAPTER THREE

HMS *Aubrietia* at War

HITLER'S WARTIME NAVAL PLAN

Hitler's plan was to control the North Atlantic Ocean, by deploying submarines (U-boats) given the task of sinking merchant ships carrying food and supplies to Britain. The U-Boats worked in groups, known as 'wolfpacks'.

Hitler's intention was to starve Britain of rations, by sinking all US and Canadian convoys crossing the North Atlantic. Up to May 1942, his plan had been working. Britain was starving.

Then, however, Britain was saved by three warships and Bletchley Park. The following story explains how all that happened.

HMS *AUBRIETIA*

HMS *Aubrietia* was part of a naval force protecting convoys of US merchant shipping vessels delivering rations and armaments to Britain. HMS *Bulldog*, a Naval destroyer, was aiding *Aubrietia* on this mission.

A single two-pounder anti-aircraft gun aboard HMCS Assiniboine, escorting a troop convoy, July 1940

A depth charge being loaded onto a depth charge thrower on another Flower-class corvette, HMS Dianthus.

Accommodation for the 85 crew members on board *Aubrietia* was very basic, but the ship was well armed. *Aubrietia* had a four-inch forward gun, a two-pounder anti-aircraft 'pom-pom' (so called because of the distinctive sound of its discharge) and four Lewis (machine) guns. Her principal weapons, however, were depth charges used to attack German submarines.

THE CAPTURE OF U-110

U-110 was on its second patrol since being commissioned, departing Lorient submarine base in Western France on 15th April 1941. On the 27th, she sank *Henri Mory* about 400 miles west of Ireland. She then successfully attacked and sank *Esmond* and *Bengore Head* east of Greenland, but the escort vessels responded. On 9th May, HMS *Aubrietia*, located the U-boat south of Iceland using ASDIC (sonar). *Aubrietia* and British destroyer *Broadway* then proceeded to drop depth charges, forcing U-110 to surface. U-110 survived the attack, but was seriously damaged.

HMS *Bulldog*, a Royal Navy destroyer, assisted *Aubrietia* in the capture of U-110, remaining in contact after *Aubrietia's* last attack. The U-boat captain, Fritz-Julius Lemp, ordered the crew to abandon ship and open the vents in order to sink the crippled U-boat. As the crew turned out onto the U-boat's deck, they came under fire from *Bulldog* and *Broadway*, the British believing the German deck gun was to be used. They ceased fire when it became clear that the U-boat was being abandoned and the crew wanted to surrender.

Lemp, however, realised that U-110 was not sinking and attempted to swim back to it to destroy certain vital equipment and paperwork on board, but he died in the attempt. 35 of the 46-crew of U-110 were rescued and locked in the hull of HMS *Bulldog*, out of sight of the following action.

HMS *Bulldog* boarding party

HMS *Bulldog* launched a whaler rowing boat (shown in the photo below) and put a boarding party aboard the submarine, led by Sub-Lieutenant David Barme. He was armed with a

pistol, but had to return it to the holster on his hip, as he needed two hands to descend the ship's vertical ladder into the submarine below. Luckily, he found the vessel totally empty.

They recovered charts, maps and books, plus what looked like a 'typewriter', which was screwed to the desk in the signals room. They were able to quickly release it from its housing and return to HMS *Bulldog* with their precious discoveries undamaged.

They had no idea what they had taken possession of and did not find out until 34 years later. In those intensive wartime months, secrecy was paramount.

The photo below shows men from HMS *Bulldog* standing on the U-Boat. The photograph was taken on board *Bulldog* by 18-year-old John Pegg, who was on lookout duty. He was unaware of the importance of the photograph until 30 years later when the top-secret documents were declassified.

John said: 'As we came in, I can recollect that the guns started firing at the part of the submarine that was above the surface. I was looking down on the submarine. It was exciting, but all we could think of was the hatred for the Germans, because they had done so much damage to the convoys.' (Extract courtesy *Plymouth Evening Herald* – 8 August 2001.)

Crew members from HMS Bulldog standing
on top of the now crippled U-110

AUBRIETIA AND *BULLDOG'S* BOOTY: THE ENIGMA MACHINE

What looked like a 'typewriter' from U-110, seen here, turned out to be the elusive German three rotor-wheel Enigma machine, a type of enciphering machine used by the German armed forces to send messages securely.

Three-wheel rotor Enigma machine

Below the three rotor wheels sits the lamp board, consisting of 26 inset lettered glass lights, then below that the keyboard consisting of the 26 typewriter keys displaying the 26 letters of the alphabet. Note there are no numeral keys 0 to 9 on Enigma; these had to be typed out in full German text. Finally, on the front of the machine sits the 'plug board', consisting of 26 paired sockets and ten plug leads, each with a double plug at each end. These cords helped to change the setting of the three rotor wheels for the oncoming 24 hours, which was known as 'setting the scrambler'. It was the three German armed forces who added the plug board to increase the machine's security. Providing the sending and receiving machine settings matched, the cypher codes worked. Throughout WWII, all German navy stations changed settings every day at midnight.

As a former qualified and working morse-coder, I can confirm that numerals 0 to 9 *do* have individual codes, yet the build of Enigma prevented their use.

The machine and accompanying documents, now in the hands of the British, were sent on to Bletchley Park, the principal centre of Allied code-breaking during the Second World War.

Alan Turing

Perhaps the most famous of the code-breakers was Alan Turing. The main focus of his was in cracking the Enigma code. Before the war, Polish mathematicians had worked out how to read Enigma messages and had shared this information with the British. The Germans increased its security at the outbreak of war by changing the cipher system daily. This made the task of understanding the code even more difficult.

Had the enemy found out that the Enigma machine from U-110 was now in the hands of the Allies, the codes would have been changed overnight. As it stood, they clearly thought that either the submarine had sunk, taking all the equipment with it, or the equipment had been destroyed by the crews prior to abandoning the ship. The Enigma codes were not changed, thus allowing the cryptanalysts at Bletchley Park to break future naval transmissions.

In 1941, Alan Turing achieved a breakthrough while working in isolation in The Cottage at Bletchley Park, depicted below in a painting by artist Steve Williams. Turing was able to discover the wiring of the rotor wheels and the naval message indicator

procedure from the catch of the large number of codebooks from U-110. Turing also managed to find a way into the Naval Enigma code and to decrypt part of the naval traffic.

WHAT BECAME OF HMS *AUBRIETIA*?

So what became of the key protagonist in this drama, HMS *Aubrietia*? The role *Aubrietia* played in the capture of U-110 ensured her place in history, but the ship saw out the rest of the war with a distinguished record. From 1941 to 1944, she saw service on convoy escort duty in the Battle of the Atlantic, the Mediterranean and North Africa.

In June 1944, *Aubrietia* came under US Navy command, joining the TG 80.6 Antisubmarine and Convoy Control Group during planned landings in the South of France. In November 1944, she returned to Royal Navy control and continued as an escort for Atlantic convoys between Freetown, the Mediterranean and Liverpool, until April 1945.

Following VE Day, *Aubrietia* was placed on the Disposal List and was sold in 1948 to Kosmos, a Norwegian company, for use as a mercantile buoy tender. *Aubrietia* was renamed *Arnfinn Bergan* and remained in service until finally being scrapped in December 1966.

CHAPTER FOUR

HMS *Petard* and the Capture of U-559

HMS *PETARD* – ROYAL NAVY DESTROYER

In 1942, a year after HMS *Aubrietia's* capture of U-110, a second, similar incident enabled a further breakthrough in the cracking of the Enigma code. HMS *Petard* (G56), pictured below, first raided and then sank a German submarine U-559 on 30th October 1942

On that date just off Port Said in the Eastern Mediterranean, four Royal Navy destroyers, one of which was HMS *Petard*, made Sonar contact with a U-boat. After a sustained depth charge attack lasting about ten hours, the U-boat was finally

forced to the surface at about 22.40. *Petard's* searchlights stabbed through the night and picked out the U-boat's conning tower which had a white donkey emblem and the numerals U-559 painted on it. The conning tower was soon struck by a shell from one of *Petard's* 4-inch guns causing the U-boat's crew to abandon ship.

Petard's first officer, Lieutenant Anthony Fasson, a likable, respected and efficient officer, stripped off, then dived into the sea followed by Able Seaman Colin Grazier and Tommy Brown, a 16-year-old canteen assistant who had lied about this age to join the Royal Navy. So many young men lied just to be at war for their country. The trio swam to the stricken U-boat and climbed down inside the conning tower to find the lights still on.

In the captain's cabin Fasson found some documents printed in water-soluble ink. Germans purposely used this type of ink as a safety feature should U-boats be captured. Despite the water pouring through the shell hole, Brown succeeded in keeping them dry as he clambered up the ladder in the conning tower and passed them to others waiting in *Petard's* whaler boat made fast alongside. Brown twice re-entered the U-boat, each time returning with more documents.

Fasson returned to the control room to wrench what looked like a radio or radar set from its fixings, but by this time the water inside the U-boat was knee-deep and rising. Brown, now on top of the conning tower, shouted down into the U-boat 'You had better come up!' as the U-boat's afterdeck was well underwater. As Grazier and Fasson started up the ladder, the U-boat suddenly sank. Brown jumped clear, but U-559 made her last dive, taking Fasson and Grazier and the unknown equipment with it.

Fasson and Grazier were each posthumously awarded the George Cross. Brown, who survived, was awarded the George Medal, but sadly he died in 1945 attempting to rescue his infant sister from a house fire.

CHAPTER FIVE

Breaking the Enigma Code

DECIPHERING CODES

During the first years of the war, Bletchley Park were decoding U-boat messages, using Turing's so-called 'Bombe' electro-mechanical machines. Bletchley name for these signals was 'SHARK'.

The first Bombe machine was initially designed in 1939 at Bletchley Park by Alan Turing with great assistance from fellow codebreaker Gordon Welchman, a Mathematician at Cambridge University, who introduced the important refinement of 'diagonal wiring'.

Gordon Welchman

Dillywn 'Dilly' Knox

The third crucial member of the team was Dillwyn 'Dilly' Knox, a British classics scholar and papyrologist at King's College, Cambridge.

Turing's Bombe device helped to significantly reduce the work of the codebreakers. Bombe machines were linked together to increase the computing power.

The first Bombe was installed at Bletchley in 1940. More copies were built, eventually totalling 211. Bombes represented the first mass-production of a specially designed cryptanalytical machine. They heralded the industrialisation of codebreaking, and the intelligence they provided was crucial to Allied success in WWII.

The photos on the next page show the relationship between the three rotor wheels of the Enigma (above) with the three rows of three rotor wheels of the Bombe (below). Each wheel corresponded to an Enigma rotor position, and this electromechanical monster – measuring 7' wide (2.1 m), 6' high (1.8 m) and 2' deep (0.6 m) – would rattle through possible settings combinations, hunting for configurations that made sense.

These photos show how the three rotor wheels of the Enigma (top) correspond to the three rows of three rotor wheels of the Bombe (bottom).

1941: CHURCHILL'S INTERVENTION

For some months during 1941, Turing and other leading codebreakers had been asking Government departments for additional staff to run the listening and decrypting stations at Bletchley Park, but without success.

On 21st October 1941, four of the leading codebreakers wrote directly to Winston Churchill, pleading for staff to assist in three areas:

The Mansion House at Bletchley Park, or 'Station X'

1   breaking Naval Enigma (Hut 8)
2   breaking Military and Air Force Enigma (Hut 6)
3   Bombe testing (Hut 6 and Hut 8).

They also requested the recruitment of WRENs to perform 8-hour shift work. On receipt of this request, Churchill messaged his Chief of Staff, General Ismay: 'Make sure they have all that they want and report back to me that this is done.'

Wrens were recruited to perform 8-hour shifts, growing to employment of over 8000 women in total.

BOMBES MASS-PRODUCED

The initial design of the British bombe was produced in 1939 at Bletchley Park by Alan Turing, with an important refinement devised by Gordon Welchman. The first working bombe was introduced in March 1940, and the second (with Welchman's refinement of 'diagonal wiring', which significantly reduced the search times) was installed in August 1940.

This build proved to be the very first British mass-produced electronic machinery. German Enigma naval messages could

not be more than 150 characters long, so that reduced the time to break the code. All Enigma messages were broken in less than 20 minutes, and a single bombe could handle two or three jobs simultaneously.

Large-scale production of the bombes was carried out by the British Tabulating Machine Company (BTM) in their factory in Letchworth (only 33 miles from Bletchley Park). In total, 211 machines were built. Only five or six bombes were housed at Station X, as Bletchley Park was known. This was for two reasons: firstly the risk of overhead bombing attacks and secondly the lack of accommodation for large numbers of Wrens.

The number of bombes sent to the five 'outstations' (each less than 40 miles from BP) were as follows: Stanmore 110 and Eastcote 80 – both stationed near London and consisting of dedicated huts to house both the bombes and the large number of WRENs (around 800 at Stanmore and at Eastcote) who worked and lived there; the three smaller sites at Wavendon, Adstock and Gayhurst each operated only five bombes. These three smaller stations were manor houses, not capable of housing more bombes or large numbers of staff. The five outstations were controlled by the Government Code and Cypher School (GC&CS) that was based in Bletchley Park

Stanmore no longer exists as a government site, having now been replaced by a housing estate.

OVERSEAS AND UK SITED 'Y' STATIONS

In addition to these five outstations, overseas and UK 'Y' stations were set up to listen to, monitor and intercept enemy wireless radio signals. They were called Y stations because of the WI in the title. German radio signals were sent by Navy, Air force and Army, as well as their secret service groups plus the railways, which also each used the Enigma machine. Each Y station was run by one of the three armed services, namely WRENs (Women's Royal Navy Service), WAAFs (Women Auxiliary Air Force) and ATS (Auxiliary Territorial Service), which in 1949 became the Women's Royal Army Corps.

Y stations were to be found in a host of oversees countries, including Malta, Cairo in Egypt, and Sarafand in Palestine, and for Japanese traffic at Abbottabad and Delhi in India, in Singapore, and later in Columbo in Ceylon (as it was known then, now Sri Lanka) and Mombasa in Kenya. Japanese sites could not use the German designed Enigma. They had to wait for a machine to arrive that allowed a Japanese character keyboard. When it did arrive, it was codenamed 'purple' by the American cryptanalysts, but the Allies still managed to break its code.

In the UK, Y stations existed in a variety of buildings and converted sites. One typical example was Beaumanor Hall in Leicestershire, shown here.

Built around 1850 by architect William Railton for the Herrick family, it remained in their possession until WWII, when it was requisitioned by the War Office. During the war it was used as a secret listening station, intercepting encrypted enemy signals, and employing 276 military men and women.

So, it is plain to see the vital role the outstations and Y stations played. Between them, they had two major services to perform. The first, at the five outstations, concerned how to handle, set up and operate the bombe machines. The second, concerning the Y stations, how to intercept, read, write down, then forward the morse code radio signals onto Bletchley Park to first decipher then translate the German plaintext into English.

Two methods of forwarding these messages were used: teleprinters, or handwritten coded messages sent to Bletchley by despatch riders. For the latter, over 200,000 motorcycles (mainly BSA M20 models) were built in the UK for both military and civilian use. For the military, both men and women (mainly WRENs, WAAFs and ATS) despatch riders, as seen here, were

Despatch riders from the Women's Royal Naval Service during WWII, receiving instruction for their next journey

deployed to carry highly secret messages to Bletchley Park. From Beaumanor to Bletchley was about 60 miles, but other stations were spread further afield, creating, at times, very long journeys by road. Even in the night, riders drove without lights to avoid enemy aircraft spotting them below. Little acknowledgement has been given to the vital services these despatch riders contributed countrywide towards Bletchley Park and its outstations and Y stations in winning the war.

1942: CHANGE OF CODES

In the spring of 1942, the Germans suddenly changed the short signal 'codes' thus blacking out all messages.

The documents retrieved from U-559 reached Bletchley Park on 24th November 1942. They proved to be the 'Short Weather Key code book' which sent the coded current weather condition. The 'Short Signal code book' sent the U-boat location at sea, its direction of travel and its speed. Each of these codes (or cribs) yielded priceless information.

The term 'crib' was used at Bletchley Park to denote any known plaintext or suspected plaintext at some point in an enciphered message.

The words shown in red above represent the German equivalent of 16 letters of the alphabet (61%) and clearly offered the greatest breakthrough of the whole campaign.

'Known words create working cribs.'

On December 13th, a crib obtained using these books made it potentially breakable on existing bombes. Six bombes were plugged up accordingly and run. Later that afternoon, following a blackout of ten months, the naval section at Bletchley Park telephoned the Admiralty's Operational Intelligence Centre to report the break-back into SHARK.

Within the next hour, the first intercept chattered off the teleprinter indicating the position of more than a dozen U-boats. A stream of intercepts followed allowing the rerouting of convoys around the waiting wolfpacks. After this breakthrough, allied shipping losses in the Atlantic were halved in January and February 1943 and, perhaps even more vitally, procedures were developed which facilitated the breaking of SHARK for the remainder of the war.

Fasson and Grazier's rescue of the two 'short signal code books' proved to be the turning point at Bletchley. It meant they were back into SHARK!

JOAN CLARKE, CRYPTANALYST

There is one more person it is important to mention for her role in the cracking of the Enigma code: Joan Clarke.

Joan Elisabeth Lowther Clarke was born on 24th June 1917 in West Norwood, London. Joan gained a double-first in Mathematics at Cambridge. Her work in an undergraduate Geometry class at Cambridge drew the attention of Gordon Welchman, who became her academic supervisor. In June 1940, Welchman recruited Clarke to the agency, where she was initially placed in an all-women group, who mainly did routine clerical work. She was quickly promoted in recognition of her workload and contributions to the team.

Miss Clarke was the only woman in Hut 8 working on the Naval Enigma Code. One of the three men working there was Alan Turing and for a brief period in 1941, she was engaged to him, but the relationship soon ended when Turing disclosed his homosexuality.

In 1947, after the war, she met and married Lieutenant-Colonel John Murray, a retired army officer who had served in India.

On 4th September 1996, Clarke died at her home in Oxford. An Oxfordshire Blue Plaque was unveiled on her house on 27th July 2019.

CHAPTER SIX

Breaking the Lorenz Code

HITLER'S LORENZ MACHINE

Hitler wanted a second machine for use solely by his High Command Generals. He approached the German electronics company, Lorenz, based in Berlin, to produce one. The Lorenz company told Hitler that their coded cipher system using an in-line attachment to teleprinters and paper tape was utterly unbreakable.

The Lorenz SZ machines had 12 wheels each with a different number of cams (or 'pins'). SZ is derived from the German *Schlüssel-Zusatz*, meaning 'cipher attachment'.

Hitler was also convinced that the Enigma was still unbreakable, proving that the secrecy maintained by the allies

The Lorenz SZ machine

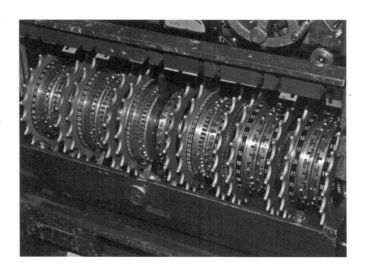

Close-up of the Lorenz SZ machine's 12 wheels, each with a different number of cams (or 'pins')

was working. Hitler was paranoid about his own people, who he was convinced were trying to betray him. Several documented attempts to end his dictatorship from within German ranks did not help, but did remove any thoughts he had about the allies breaking his crypted messaging systems.

LORENZ CYPHER CODE BROKEN

The Lorenz cipher system was worked on at Bletchley Park by mathematicians Max Newman, Brigadier John Tiltman and young Chemistry graduate Bill Tutte (pictured below).

Max Newman   *Brigadier John Tiltman*   *Bill Tutte*

Tiltman and Tutte's greatest achievement was to establish the internal structure of the German Lorenz enciphered teleprinter (called 'TUNNY' by the Bletchley teams), and used by the German Generals to transmit high-level coded messages.

These two codebreakers solved the mathematical problems in 1942 before ever seeing the Lorenz machine! The initial 'mock-up' of the 12-wheel cipher system built at Bletchley Park was initially called 'Heath Robinson' after the cartoonist designer of fantastic machines. Such was the humour that penetrated within the ranks of the codebreakers!

However, on 30th August 1941, the German operators of the Lorenz system made a terrible – but to the code-breakers, invaluable – mistake. The German sending station, after sending a 4000-character message, was instructed, by radio, by the receiving station, with the German equivalent of 'Didn't get that, send it again!' The sender did not change the original machine start positions, which was strictly forbidden, and what's more, used many abbreviations on the second run. He was clearly annoyed at this request and as such, took short-cuts.

This gave the codebreakers access into solving the Lorenz cipher. It took 10 days to accomplish, but break the code they did!

The main contribution of the third key figure, Max Newman, was in producing a functional specification of machinery ('Heath Robinson' and Colossus) that was used to determine the settings of the Lorenz Machine's wheels.

LORENZ TELEPRINTER CODED MACHINE

Tommy Flowers, pictured on the next page – a brilliant Post Office Electronics Engineer – built the Lorenz teleprinter cipher machine, following the earlier groundwork performed by Newman, Tiltman and Tutte in breaking the code.

Tommy Flowers

Teleprinters are not based on the 26-letter alphabet and do not use Morse code on which Enigma depended. Teleprinters use the 32-symbol Baudot code, a binary code using crosses and dots and sent on punched paper tape. Flowers called his machine 'Colossus' after its switch-on in April 1944 – six months before the end of World War II.

The truth is that Heath Robinson and ten Colossus computers between them, deciphered 13,508 Lorenz messages at Bletchley Park from November 1942 to 8 May 1945. The deciphered Lorenz messages made one of the most significant contributions to British military intelligence and because of the high-level strategic nature of the information contained in the decoded messages.

BLETCHLEY LINGUISTIC DEPARTMENT

Captain Raymond C. 'Jerry' Roberts worked at Bletchley Park from 1941 to 1945. He was a founding member of the linguistic department, working on translating all German messages on both the Enigma and the Lorenz cipher systems. He was affectionally nicknamed 'Jerry', because of his role at Bletchley Park.

Raymond 'Jerry' Roberts

The linguistic group he was a key part of were not only translating German messages taken and read at Bletchley, but also those sent on from the five outstations to Bletchley Park. All the German to English translations were performed at Bletchley only. This required all of the five outstations to send German 'plain text' message they had deciphered on to Bletchley for translating into English. This was yet another security procedure they adopted and maintained.

'Jerry' was the longest surviving Bletchley-ite, living till the age of 93. There are many online videos featuring him with his distinctive 'croaky' voice. He was awarded the MBE by the late Queen Elizabeth II, and a stamp was printed with his face on as a tribute to his wartime contributions. The stamps are only available at the Bletchley Park Post Office.

HMS *BULLDOG'S* LAST WARTIME SERVICE

On VE Day, 8th May 1945, HMS *Bulldog* and HMS *Beagle* sailed to St Peter Port in Guernsey to assist in the liberation of the Channel Islands (the port is shown here in two contrasting photos – one modern and one from during the German occupation). The document of surrender of the

Top: St Peter Port in Guernsey during the period of German occupation during WWII. Hitler was keen to produce images like this showing German soldiers on 'British territory'.

Bottom: This image shows the same harbour view as it appears today – the centre of the town being relatively unchanged.

occupying German garrisons was signed on board *Bulldog* in the harbour on the 9th May – exactly four years to the day after the capture of U-110. This must have been a momentous occasion for the captain and crew of *Bulldog*.

The refugee children based in Horsforth could now go home, in some cases after five years' separation from their parents. What stories they would have had to tell about the Yorkshire village and the families they lived with!

THE FINAL OUTCOME

Breaking first Enigma, then Lorenz, shortened the war by two years, it is estimated, saving some 14 million lives.

ULTRA was the UK Government code name for all Bletchley findings, derived from GCHQ classification – 'Very secret' or 'Ultra secret'.

Winston Churchill insisted on assigning names to special wartime operations, such as 'Operation Dynamo' the Dunkirk evacuation. Now 'Operation Ultra' was used for information sent from Bletchley Park. Churchill once said to King George VI: 'It was thanks to Ultra that we won the war.'

Sometime, following a visit to Bletchley, Churchill called Bletchley Park:

> **'the geese who laid the golden eggs and never cackled.'**

This quote refers first to the team's codebreaking achievements, but also to the fact that the 9000+employees maintained a rigid silence throughout the war.

Today we add those brave men of HMS *Aubrietia*, HMS *Bulldog* and HMS *Petard*, who between them, captured the equipment and the vital code books which helped the Bletchley codebreakers, and Britain, end the war.

CHAPTER SEVEN

After the War – Colossus Rebuilt

DESTRUCTION OF COLOSSUS

After close of war in 1945, eight Colossus machines at Bletchley Park were torn apart and two were sent to Eastcote in North London, then to GCHQ in Cheltenham. These two were also torn apart in 1960, and any drawings of Colossus were also burnt, in order to keep the Colossus a wartime secret.

In the 1990s, new information about Colossus re-emerged, and a movement to rebuild a replica machine was started by Bletchley Park's computer scientist and curator, Tony Sale.

THE COLOSSUS REBUILD PROJECT

In 1993, Tony was able to gather together all the information available. This included eight wartime photographs taken of Colossus in 1945 plus some fragments of circuit diagrams that some engineers had kept, albeit illegally!

In June 1994, Tony visited Dr Allen Coombs, who had engineered the Mk 2 Colossus from Tommy Flowers' Mk 1. He kindly gave Tony all his wartime notes, including some circuit diagrams of Colossus. This generous gift helped make the rebuild possible. The aim of the project was to rebuild Colossus in its historic environment – in one room in Block H where Colossus No 9 had stood during the war.

The replica Colossus machine built at Bletchley Park

The photograph above shows the replica Colossus once it had finally been put together.

To the far right we see the 'bedstead' which houses the paper tapes. It's called the bedstead because it has the physical size and shape of a single bed.

Colossus was originally built at the Post Office Research Laboratories in North London, and much of the equipment is standard Post Office (now BT) telephone equipment of relays and selectors as found in a standard Strowger exchange of the period, also known as 'Step-by-Step' (SXS). As Tony recalls, a large number of old Post Office telephone exchanges were being decommissioned and changed to digital, which meant Tony was able to collect large amounts of equipment which otherwise would just have gone for scrap.

A key feature of Colossus is that is was powered by valves. Tony Sale managed to find enough supplies of valves and build a 'slow, power-up-circuit' to protect them from burn-out. Valves are not capable of receiving mains power switch-on as it causes them to 'blow'. However, if the mains current is slowly built up, valves cope thereafter. To get round this, Tony's 'power-up circuit' did that job.

A fascinating account of the Colossus rebuild, written by Tony Sale, is still available on the National Museum of Computing website, at tnmoc.org/rebuilding-colossus

ROYAL OPENING

The official Royal Opening of Colossus 2 took place on 6th June 1996. The photograph shows His Royal Highness The Duke of Kent switching on the replica flanked by Tommy Flowers (seated) and Tony Sale, the builder. What a privilege the occasion must have been for Flowers, after seeing his initial Colossus help shorten the war and now living to witness its rebuild. He was 91 when this picture was taken, hence his being seated in the Duke's presence. He died 2 years later.

HRH The Duke of Kent switches on the replical Colossus

PERSONAL CONNECTIONS

Who is Tony Sale? He can be seen right on the picture, alongside another BP Engineer.

I first met Tony in 1989 in a pub in London. In that year I was then responsible for managing the installation of BT's first national computer system. On the last Friday of each month, I had to report progress on the installation to BT's then General Manager, Derek Denyer, who then passed my report to the BT Board of Directors.

*Tony Sale (right) with another BP Engineer
working on the Colossus rebuild*

Tony and I met regularly on these Friday lunchtimes, and he led me to believe that he was working at Holborn Telephone Exchange down the road. He was particularly keen to hear about the computer system and hardware I was installing. Naturally, I was equally keen to share what I was able. I was to learn later how and why Tony was professionally skilled at 'friendly' deception!

I took early retirement at the end of that year.

On 30th July 2007 I re-visited Bletchley Park to attend a lecture, and entering Block H (former Hut 8), I saw the Colossus computer for the first time. A voice behind me said: 'What are you doing here Jack?' It was Tony!

Tony Sale spent his formative years as the leading Computer Scientist for 'MI5'. In 1991, he got involved with Bletchley Park. He and his wife Margaret personally funded the cost of rebuilding Colossus and they also set up the Bletchley Park Trust, which still exists today. Tony proudly told me that he and his wife were affectionately known as 'Mr & Mrs Bletchley' by all their fellow workers.

Tony Sale appears in the credits of the 2001 UK film *Enigma*, as the 'Technical Advisor'. The film *Enigma* also talks about Fasson and Grazier recovering the code books thus allowing the 'SHARK' code to be broken again. While that part of the

Tony Sale, 'Mr Bletchley'

film is true, the characters names in the film are all fictitious.

In the 2014 film *The Imitation Game*, all the characters' names are true, with Alan Turing being played by Benedict Cumberbatch, alongside Keira Knightley as Joan Clarke. Most of the storyline about building the Bombe and breaking the Enigma code is accurate, except the scriptwriters claim that all that was needed to break the code was to know the words 'weather' and 'Heil bloody Hitler'. While, as you have read, weather was a crucial crib, the claim about 'Hitler' was a filmmaker's 'catchphrase' to make viewers remember it. They also imply it was a small team that worked at Bletchley, whereas, in reality, the staffing level was on an industrial scale. Regrettably, Dilly Knox, Gordon Welchman Max Newman, John Tiltman and Bill Tutte do not feature at all.

Sadly, Tony Sale died 28th August 2011. It was not till after his death that I found out about his top-secret employment. He was the ultimate professional, but for me, for ever, a dear friend.

COLOSSUS – CLOSELY GUARDED SECRET

In 1996, the Americans celebrated the 50th anniversary of the switch on of ENIAC (Electronic Numerical Integrator and Calculator), claiming it was the world's first electronic digital calculator. This myth arose because Colossus had been successfully hidden in secrecy for so many years. Tony Sale made sure his replica copy of Colossus was ready and switched on at Bletchley Park, just as the original was in 1944, two years before ENIAC.

There has been a tight-lipped silence from across the water ever since!

CHAPTER EIGHT

U-571 –
History Rewritten

HISTORICAL EVENTS REINTERPRETED ...

In 2000, Universal Pictures released a submarine film called *U-571*, starring Matthew McConaughey and Harvey Keitel, among others. The film tells the story of a World War II German submarine boarded by American submariners who capture her Enigma cipher machine.

Two credits are given at the end of the film.

- 'May 9, 1941 Enigma machine and coding documents captured from U-110 by HMS *Bulldog* and HMS *Aubrietia* of the 3rd Escort Group, Royal Navy.'
- 'October 30, 1942 Short weather cipher captured from U-559 by HMS *Petard* of the Royal Navy.'

The UK government wrote to the US complaining about the blatantly misleading premise of the film, stating that USA were not even in the war in May 1941, when HMS *Aubrietia* forced U-110 to the surface and recovered the Enigma machine. USA joined the Allies following the Japanese attack on Pearl Harbor in December 1941. The year after, HMS *Petard* recovered the code books from U-559.

In response, a letter signed by President Bill Clinton, was received by MP Paul Truswell at the House of Commons, London SW1A. (Paul Truswell was then MP for Pudsey in West Yorkshire, the constituency that includes Horsforth.) The letter read as follows:

Dear Mr Truswell,

Thank you for your letter concerning the Universal Studios film 'U-571'. I understand your desire to see the role of the Royal Navy and the HMS *Aubrietia* acknowledged. As you know, Universal Studios has stated that the film is not intended to be an accurate portrayal of historical events.

I have the honor of participating in several ceremonies marking the 50th anniversary of World War II. The Royal Navy's capture of U-110 and the recovery of its 'Enigma' encoding machine were of momentous importance to the course of the war and enabled Allied codebreakers to decipher a vast number of encoded German messages. Many historians familiar with these achievements believe they helped turn the tide against Nazi Germany and may have shortened the war considerably.

The citizens of Horsforth can take great pride in having raised the funds to purchase HMS *Aubrietia*, the Royal Navy corvette that forced U-110 to the surface. The Royal Navy's action undoubtedly saved thousands of Allied lives and serves as an inspiration for future generations.

Again, thank you for writing on this important, historical matter.

Sincerely

Bill Clinton

CHAPTER NINE

Morse code

THE INVENTION OF MORSE CODE

Morse code has played an important part in the events I describe in this book. During World War II, the Germans used Morse code to transmit millions of military field messages, after having enciphered them using their Enigma machines.

The Code was invented in the 1830s by the American Samuel Finley Breese Morse (1791–1872), an inventor and painter. The code is a system whereby letters of the alphabet, numerals and punctuation marks are represented by an arrangement of dots, dashes and spaces, which can be transmitted by telegraphy.

Self-portait by Samuel Morse, c.1812

MY EXPERIENCE OF USING MORSE CODE

During my three years in the RAF, I was trained in Morse code signalling, as well as the theories, and the designing and building, of telephone and telegraph circuits. In the exam at the end of the course, I achieved a 100% pass mark. This led to further advanced training in Direction Finding at Bletchley Park, where I was trained to install and use a 'Radio Goniometer Aerial System'.

I still have my handwritten notebook on the initial Morse code, Telephony and Telegraphy course held at RAF Compton Bassett in 1958.

I was posted to Germany during the 'Cold War' taking down coded messages and taking bearings on Russian Army units. The Morse transmissions I was listening to were all gobbledygook to me, and I never did find out what all the coded messages meant!

Finally, to give you a flavour of what a code looks like and how it can be used is as follows.

At the end of every 8-hour shift in Germany and after listening to endless messages, the one 'code set' I longed to hear was the sign-off code, meaning you could put down your pen, remove your headset and leave your post. To sign off in Morse code, the international word for goodbye is the French phrase *Au revoir*. However, that is shortened to just four letters:

A R V A

Translated into Morse code that comes out as:

A .-
R .-.
V ...-
A .-

To speak this, Morse coders do not say 'dot dash' they say 'di da'. So to sign off shift we receive this code:

di da   di da di   di di di da   di da

Now as I close this book, some sixty-two years since I last listened to and transmitted Morse code, this is the one signal I shall remember to my dying day.

CHAPTER TEN

Bibliography and resources

PREVIOUS BOOKS AND ARTICLES BY THE AUTHOR

Books

Metcalfe, Jack & Apps, John (2003) *The Marquetry Course*. Published by Batsford, London UK.

Metcalfe, Jack (2018) *Chippendale's classic Marquetry Revealed*. Published by Jack Metcalfe and now available on Amazon.

Metcalfe, Jack & Apps, John (2020) *The classic Marquetry Course*. Published by Jack Metcalfe. Replacing the Batsford publication above and now available on Amazon.

Metcalfe, Jack (2022) *Finding & Naming Thomas Chippendale's Marquetry Team*. Published by Jack Metcalfe and available on Amazon.

Metcalfe, Jack (2021) *The Warrington Chest 1888* (Chapter 4, 'Marquetry'). Published and supplied by Tools and Trade History Society (TATHS)

Metcalfe, Jack (2020) trans. Hans Michaelsen *Die Kunst des Holzfärbens* ('The Art of Wood Dyeing – synthetic dyestuffs versus historical wood stains').

Article

Metcalfe, Jack (2009) 'A Chippendale Tribute to the Lunar Society', *The Furniture History Society – Newsletter* No. 176, November 2009, pp. 1–5.

OTHER RESOURCES

Peter A. Watson (2011) *From Atlantic to Station X,* Horsforth Village Historical Society, Registered Charity No 517198 (out of print). This book has now been renamed and replaced by *HMS Aubrietia: The Horsforth Ship*, written by Beryl Biggins, and is available on Amazon worldwide.

Sale, Tony, 'Rebuilding Colossus', www.tnmoc.org/rebuilding-colossus, article about the Colossus Rebuild Project on the National Museum of Computing website.

Welchman, Gordon (1997, 2nd edition), *The Hut Six Story: Breaking the Enigma Codes*, M.&M. Baldwin.

Index